Content Creation

BOOK DESCRIPTION

Great content helps to build your brand. It also helps in establishing your authority in the given domain. (Who doesn't prefer buying from an expert who knows everything about a particular niche?) A strong content strategy creates sufficient interest in and awareness of your product. Integrating content into the sales process makes it all the more efficient than simply pushing your product on the customer. It makes your brand comes across as likable, relatable, identifiable and human. No one likes to be sold to by bots. Buyers love to buy from real humans with whom they can establish connections. And what better way to establish a dialogue with people than giving them valuable and powerful content that has the potential to impact their lives?

A strong, clear and consistent content strategy helps you build a following of loyal customers who make repeat purchases from you. You do not just make new customers; you also retain the existing ones by offering them sheer value.

Let's dive head first into this fascinating world of content marketing, and begin to master content creation to put your blog on the highway to success.

Enjoy reading.

CONTENTS

Content Creation 1

Introduction 6

Why Do You Need a Plan? 9

Planning Basics 12

Planning Tips to Make Things Easier 20

Your Guide to Content Planning Success 23

Why Do You Need Consistent Content? 28

Content Creation Basics 31

Creation Tips You Need to Know 35

Your Guide to Content Creation Success 42

Content Automation/Scheduling Basics 50

Scheduling/Automation Tips You Need to Know 57

Your Guide to Content Scheduling Success 60

Why Is Creating Content Important? 63

Content Writing Tips 69

Conclusion 89

Introduction

You have a blog and are active on Social Media. You post often, ok most of the time…

To be really honest, you haven't posted anything worthwhile in a long time.

It's just so hard to keep a consistent flow of content going on a daily or weekly basis. You found inspiration today and created a masterpiece but there is no way you can repeat that weekly.

You need some sort of strategy to make it work.

This is what this book is all about, giving you a plan not only to create your content but also to automate the publishing.

By the end of this content creation strategy guide you will know the best way to

- Plan for great content
- Create quality content
- Use scheduling tools to automate your publishing and make engagement easy
- And much more

PART 1: CONTENT PLANNING

WHY DO YOU NEED A PLAN?

You should never approach social media or blog post writing with the idea that you can just fly by the seat of your pants. Planning is extremely important to transform occasional content creation into focused content marketing.

Always try to plan out at least 12 weeks of content so that you will have a clear idea on how your content will tie in with your marketing, sales and ultimate business goals for the months ahead.

It will be much easier to be more consistent when you have your content all planned out or even created and scheduled and, as we know, consistent content creation is really the key to social media success.

Planned content also makes it a lot easier to travel or take some time off from your business as your content is already planned out, created and scheduled and you will still get a constant stream of traffic and income even though you are not physically present.

Planning helps you schedule blocks of time to create in bulk, which saves you immense time in the long run. We all have heard how much time we lose switching between different tasks and, unfortunately, with something like blog posting and social media there are a tremendous number of different tasks that needs to be done, such as:

- Getting themes
- Creating images
- Writing posts
- Posting or scheduling posts
- Sharing these posts on social media

If you plan it right you can get consistent income from your SM traffic to your opt-in pages and/or specific sales pages. Just use a combination of value adding and promotional posts aimed at the specific product you are promoting.

Another benefit of planning and scheduling ahead of time is that it opens up your calendar to life interaction and engagement with your audience. You can answer questions and engage on a personal level without having to worry about getting new content out.

Finally, you can plan to publish your content at the optimal times for your specific audience no matter which time zone you or your audience are located in.

When you use an editorial calendar and plan as suggested, you will always be in control of your content marketing.

PLANNING BASICS

Every blogger, social media marketer or online entrepreneur needs to know the content planning basics that will help you attract clients consistently with your great content.

These basics will prevent you from getting overwhelmed with all the little details. So, if you feel you are not organized enough to plan for 12 weeks ahead, then read this immediately so you understand the fundamentals critical to your content planning efforts.

Fundamental #1 Planning for Consistent Content

Content is the fundamental building block of every successful digital business.

One of the biggest mistakes people are making in their social media strategy is not to have consistent content. It is also one of the things that can cause the most stress in your business. You know that you have to publish content regularly to keep your clients engaged and to provide value. But when you sit there daily, thinking what you should post, it becomes a huge headache. Social media is one of the best ways to make personal connections with clients and can drive a ton of traffic to your sites and pages if done correctly. It is therefore imperative that your plan includes consistent content on every platform you choose to engage in. By following the strategies in the rest of the book you will never need to worry about this again.

Fundamental #2 Using the Correct Tools to Plan

It doesn't really matter what tools you use to plan your content as long as it includes the components you need. Firstly, you want to be able to have a clear calendar view of what is coming up for the following weeks, month or several weeks. You need to be able to add important dates for business, holidays and any events that will influence your content.

You need to be able to add your ideas and resources, but this can also be done in a separate tool. You then need to have a space for each platform you want to engage in, with enough space to add your themes or topics. If you need to engage on a platform more than once a day, you need to be able to show that.

Remember that a lot of your posts will be shared on multiple platforms so create a system around that.

Having a written-out plan for what is coming up is crucial for content planning success; without one you are creating content blindly and may very well find that you get overwhelmed or lost.

I like to use a pen and paper and have created a simple editorial calendar for this use, you can download it over here. Other good options are online calendars like Google calendar or you can plan directly into your online scheduling tool like CoScedule or eClincher.

Fundamental #3: Knowing the Different Categories of Posts

There are basically 5 different categories when it comes to social media and blog posts. Having a good blend of these categories makes for more interesting, informative and convertible content.

Educational

This category is all posts that are informative in nature. You can share tips, tricks, how-to videos, resources, lists and any other content that teaches your ideal client something in your niche. This is mainly posts that you created but can also be something someone else created that might be interesting for your audience, as long as you solve any problems your ideal client might have. I normally tend to classify posts from other people under the entertainment category, but this is totally up to you.

Inspirational

Inspirational posts can be quote posts or quote images or posts about a story or video that will motivate your audience. You can share something about yourself or other people. These thoughtful posts can increase interest and discussion. You can write an inspirational story about your opinions on an event, your employees' or clients' accomplishments or your company's philosophy.

Entertaining

Entertainment posts are normally posts that have nothing to do with your business. It can be anything that your ideal client will find entertaining and useful. These can include jokes or timely and comical photos. Anything that is funny or clever can be entertaining to your audience. Just keep in mind that humor can be quite tricky and does not work for all types of businesses. It is for this reason that I include educational content from other people that might be entertaining for my audience as well.

Engaging

Here you can have any type of post that increases engagement, gets everyone involved and creates conversation. You can ask questions (short answers), answer questions, have office hours, contests or challenges.

You can also give them a peek behind your business or life by posting photos of your new office, project planning or other tools, photo shoots, book covers and testimonials.

Other interesting options are "caption the image", "fill in the blank" or "either or question" posts to help get people talking.

Promotional

The final category includes all promotional posts. All advertisements for products, programs and services. Posts can promote your freebies or other free products; webinars, events, other social media platforms and websites.

Promoting jv partners or affiliates also falls under this category. Promotional posts should be last on your list of priorities as people need to engage with you and know you before they will buy from you.

It is important to understand these categories before you start your planning. You need to keep to the rule of posting about 20% of your content in each of these categories. So, basically, equal amounts in each category. If any of the categories do not fell feel right for your business you don't need to use them but just always keep to the 80-20 rule where you post 80% non-promotional and 20% promotional posts.

Using a tool like Meet Edgar or eClincher, where you can automate your postings in each of these categories, can be a great help to keep your content consistent. Gary Vanynerchuck's book, *Jab Jab Jab Right Hook*, is also a great read if you are serious about using social media for your content marketing efforts.

Fundamental #4: Deciding on the Platforms You Want to Engage In

You don't need to be active on all the social media platforms. The best thing is to figure out where your ideal clients are spending their time. Are they on Facebook in specific groups? Will images on Pinterest or Instagram get their attention? Or are they looking for specific answers to their problem on YouTube? For business to business companies it might be better to make connections on LinkedIn.

There might be fewer of your ideal clients on article sharing sites or SlideShare but the competition might be less fierce.

The other thing to take into consideration is the saturation of the market. For instance, Facebook is quite saturated; people are used to ads and don't get excited over most stuff but YouTube is still very cost effective and Instagram paid advertising is brand new at this stage, so also keep that in mind.

You will get very overwhelmed if you try to be sufficiently active on all the platforms. It is best to start off by concentrating on two or three of the best platforms for your specific niche.

Fundamental #5: Deciding on the Amount of Times You Want to Engage on Each Platform and Keeping It Consistent

You need to decide how much you are willing to engage on each platform. There are optimal amounts of times for each platform, but it is more important that you keep your engagement consistent. You can use the following as a guide and then plan how much you can or want to post to each platform.

The optimal amount of engagement to **Facebook** is 2 posts a day. That is 2 posts to either your personal profile or a Facebook page. Of course, you can still post to different groups.

For **Twitter** it is between 3 and 5 times per day. Engagement does drop off after 3 times, so for a start, 3 times a day might be better.

You need to post to **Instagram** twice a day or more. As long as you stay consistent in the number of posts you make there will be no drop off in engagements.

For **Pinterest** you need to pin 5 times a day or more. There is no drop off in engagement after 5 posts.

The maximum or optimal amount of times to post to **LinkedIn** is once a day for every week day. No more than 20 times a month.

Post to **Google+** 3 times a day at most, consistency is very important. You will get a decrease in traffic up to 50% if your frequency wanes.

Blog at least 2x a week. You can double your lead by increasing your monthly blog posts from 4 times to 6-8 times.

Start off with fewer posts to fewer platforms and increase over time. As stated before, it is more important to stay consistent. So, decide on a realistic amount and plan accordingly.

Now that you know the importance of these 5 fundamentals, it is time to move on to the actual steps you need to take.

PLANNING TIPS TO MAKE THINGS EASIER

Here are a few tips to help bloggers, social media marketers or online entrepreneurs to plan for even better content, more engagement from clients and a consistent income from their efforts.

Content Planning Tip #1: You need to block out your time for planning

You need to plan to plan… For most of the things in this book you need a block of time set out to do things in bulk. When focusing on one thing only, you will be much more productive and excellent. Therefore, it is vital that you schedule this in your diary. Decide how often you are going to plan and for how long. Either do it once a month or once every 12 weeks. Even if it takes a chuck of your time, you will save a great deal of time in the long run. Do it now; grab your diary or calendar and schedule in your next planning session.

Content Planning Tip #2: Re-Using content

When creating content for social media and other platforms, you need to keep in mind in what ways you can re-use this content on as many platforms as possible.

The format of the post on different platforms might vary a little and the sizes of the images might change, but the core of your article can be used on all these platforms. This will increase your reach and productivity.

I will go into more detail in the next part on content creation, but keep in mind that an article can easily be converted into a PowerPoint or Keynote presentation. You can turn this into videos by adding your voiceover. You can transcribe your audio into podcasts and interviews to create articles. Or you can just take different parts of your article and tweet or post it on Facebook or add it to photos to create lovely image posts.

Content Planning Tip #3: Plan for live engagement as well

When you create your plan, remember to schedule time for daily live engagement. You won't need a lot of time as all of your posts will already be scheduled to be published. Just have a few minutes a day where you can answer questions, like or retweet/repost posts and follow new people. Also, if you have specific themes in groups that you want to participate in on certain days, mark it on your calendar so that you won't forget. You will not need to spend all of your time on your social media platforms, especially not if you use a tool like eClincher where you can monitor and engage on all platforms from within one tool.

Content Planning Tip #4: Using colors

Here is a fun extra tip. When creating your calendar on paper or when using a calendar tool like Google Calendar, have your different categories in different colors (create a calendar for each category in Google Calendar). This will give you a good overview to see if you have enough posts in each category or if some of the categories are overshadowing, especially if the promotional category is excessive.

You can also use colors for different platforms but keep it as simple as possible. You don't want to make it too confusing. It needs to be very straightforward and clear. When it is fun, easy to use and simple to see what is going on, you will use it more.

YOUR GUIDE TO CONTENT PLANNING SUCCESS

These are the simple steps you need to take to plan your content calendar easily.

Step #1: Grab your sales and marketing calendar, holiday and special event calendar and start planning around that

To plan your content for the following weeks you need to know what's happening in your business and around you in the world.

Timely content is more engaging, so around holidays and big events posting about it can increase your reach and comments.

It is always more effective if your non-promotional ties in with your promotional content. Therefore, if you have something big coming up, like a launch or an event, let your non-promotional content spark the interest on the subject.

Once you have marked these dates, you need to start investigating your themes for the weeks…

Step #2: Start to investigate your themes

It is up to you how you organize your themes. You might have a different theme weekly or monthly or have the same theme for 5 weeks tying it all together in the 6th week.

Again, this will depend on what is going on in your business and might be different around launch dates and big events. I like to have a theme for a month, more or less focusing on what I plan to release or work on in that month.

Once you have decided on your frequency you can investigate different themes in your niche if needed.

The three best ways to find interesting topics in your niche are:

Visit Forums in Your Niche

Search for forums in your niche on Google. A good idea is to order the topics by the amount of comments or replies. All the most popular topics will be at the top. You can also use this to get good headline ideas.

Go to iTunes and Look into Podcasts in Your Niche

There are 1000s of podcasts with lots of episodes in each of them. Look for podcasts in your niche and find episodes with plenty of downloads. Again, this will be a good indication of what people want to know about in your niche.

On Amazon Search for Books in Your Niche

People go to Amazon to buy mostly. When you investigate topics in your area you can easily see what people are willing to pay for. Use the "Look Inside" facility of books with high rankings in the categories of your interest. Have a look at the Table of Contents and you will swiftly find interesting topics.

Note all the popular themes on each of these platforms by looking at the comments, downloads and ranking. You will find a trend and also find interesting topics or themes that you might not have thought of. You can then eliminate themes that won't work for your upcoming weeks or move them to a someday-maybe list.

Having themes planned out is already a huge step in simplifying your planning.

Step #3: Start to Fill in Your Calendar

With the different themes handy, now start to plan topics for posts in each of the social media platforms that you've decided to engage in.

This is still just planning so you don't need to know exactly what you are going to write, but keep in mind the fundamentals: What topics are you going to write for each category? How many times are you going to post to each platform and which platforms?

Remember that a lot of the times you are going to repost to more than one social media platform if the topic is relevant. Mark this on your calendar as well.

Make this your own and make it fun. If you like pen and paper, use a printable editorial calendar and colored pens. If you like techy tools on your iPad or computer, use them. It doesn't matter. As long as you plan it out and the plan works for you.

PART 2: CONTENT CREATION

WHY DO YOU NEED CONSISTENT CONTENT?

When you use an editorial calendar and plan, as suggested, you will always be in control of your content marketing. With your strategy prepared you are now ready to start creating your content. Before you dive in, however, let's quickly have an overview of why it is important to create content on a consistent basis.

We already know that content marketing is one of the only marketing techniques that is still surviving. Consumers have started to cut out, ignore and simply hate any other type of marketing and will—if not able to cut it out completely—simply just switch off when faced with these types of ads.

Given this, it is therefore important to focus our marketing efforts on content marketing and social media marketing and do everything in our ability to improve the quality and consistency of these postings. You need to build a relationship with your future client and this can only be done by providing content that they really want to read. Once they have found you and decided that what you offer is what they want, they will start looking forward to your posts. This is exactly what you want. This excitement over your content will, however, only happen if they have something to look forward to on a pre-informed basis.

It is important to build your authority in your niche so that you stand out from the crowd and are recognized in your field. You will get nowhere by just copying the work of another writer. To stand out from the crowd, you need to use your own voice and ideas. Doing this will help people notice you and help them see that you have your own ideas and creativity. This will build trust in your readers and they will turn to you for new information.

Search Engine Optimization is an important one. Without a search engine, you may not even be found! To help with SEO, try using specific key words to the topic you are discussing. The more important keywords you use and the more you use them the easier it will be for people to find and come to you. There are some websites that will offer specific keywords for you to use when talking about your subject. The more consistently you create content the more your site gets crawled, the more your posts get shared and it's all the better for SEO.

Going viral can be a hard thing to achieve and many times it can happen completely by accident. Other times it feels like it's a flash in the pan and then it's gone. Both of which can and have happened. Because of this, you want to go viral because of something positive rather than something negative that can hinder you for a very long time.

To help with going viral, try writing about current topics and give your opinions on them. Be unique when doing your writing and don't be afraid to go slightly outside of your comfort zone.

You can't force something to go viral, but you can try creative new things and ideas when writing your entries. Get creative and unique so that you stand out from the crowd and encourage people to share your posts and images.

CONTENT CREATION BASICS

Before we go into the details of how to create valuable content on a consistent basis, let's look at the basic fundamentals that every online marketer or digital entrepreneur should know to ensure that the created content is of a high quality and an asset to your brand.

Fundamental #1: Know who you are writing for

Who do you want to reach with your content? Who is your ideal client? This may differ from content piece to content piece or you might have an exact client avatar that you always speak to. You should, however, consider this before starting work on your content. Know who you want to reach and the type of language that you have to use to attract them.

This is important because if you are vague with your message it might not be heard by the right people. Remember if you are trying to appeal to everyone you will appeal to no one. Once you have considered who you want to reach, listen to their conversations by being in the same groups or forums that they are in. You can even read reviews on Amazon or Itunes to figure out what pain points or concerns they have.

Knowing who your ideal client is will also help you decide which platforms to post the specific piece of content to as certain types of clients will be on certain platforms.

Fundamental #2: What is your goal for your content creation?

It is important to decide why you are creating a specific piece of content. Are you trying to establish credibility or authority on a subject? Is your sole goal to attract leads or traffic to your website or to make a sale? Every piece of content should have an end goal.

Make sure that the content you create conveys that message. Also, having an overall goal for your social media in general ensures that your top-level goal, as well as your secondary goals, will be supported by the content you create.

Why is this important for Content Creation success?

Having an end goal in mind will help you with your strategy and keep you on target, it will also make content creation easier as you will have an idea of the message you want to bring to them.

Fundamental #3: Scheduling big chunks of time to create your content in bulk

You need to create space for creating in bulk. As mentioned before in the planning section, doing things in bulk and in blocks of time increases your productivity enormously. Create outlines and headlines in bulk; write, search for photos or design your images all in bulk.

Writing post by post without having any strategy will drain you and will be extremely difficult to sustain. Schedule your time; for example, Mondays you could create the outline for 6 posts. Tuesday and Wednesday, you write 3 posts. Thursday you search for and design 6 blog post images and Friday you schedule them all. Or take one weekend a month and do it all. Find whatever works best for you.

Fundamental #4: Creating great images with consistent branding in the correct sizes across platforms

It is important to have the correct sizes for each platform because images created for one platform might be cut off or stretched in another platform.

Your image needs to be consistent with your branding across all platforms. The more attention you receive for this particular brand the more people will be drawn to you. Stay with your style of images and use consistent fonts.

Always be sure to add your website address or logo to images and keep the placement uniform for all images.

You can even digitally insert quotes from your articles into your high-quality images. Once this is done, you can share them on Facebook, Twitter, Instagram, Pinterest, and any other image sharing sites you can think of.

CREATION TIPS YOU NEED TO KNOW

With the fundamentals in place let's have a look at some tips to help you create unique content fast and efficiently.

Content Creation Tip #1: Create quality content that speaks to your audience and addresses their pain points

As mentioned before, when writing up information for your audience you need to know exactly who you are talking to. But you also need to address their pain points in a clear and direct way. To avoid ending up on a wild tangent, it is important to list out the main pain points that you wish to address.

Through addressing the right pain points, you will be able to write a very powerful entry for the right blog and/or audience. You will be able to create content that helps the intended audience identify with your words and give the impression that you are speaking to them directly, being there to solve their problems.

When giving your information, it is more important to be honest with the intended audience than positive all the time. If the audience feels that you are withholding something they may lose interest in what you have to say.

Don't skip here and there on any topics that you may feel may be important.

A good idea that many people choose to use when discussing points is to have five important points and then wrap it up in the sixth point. This means have five important things in a list that you wish to bring up and discuss. The sixth point is more of a conclusion that wraps it all up. This way you give people the information that they need, and the entry is not too long.

If you want to do longer reports or e-books, you can have ten to twelve overhead themes and then identify ten important topics beneath each of them.

Content Creation Tip #2: Create content fast with the help of templates and techniques

Templates can really be your friends as they take away the whole "staring at a blank page" feeling. You can create your own templates from previous blog posts or download them for free or a small fee.

You get templates for the different types of posts that I will go into more detail about later, but just to give you an idea these can be, for example, FAQ type templates, "Tip post" templates or "How to do" something templates.

Templates are also very useful as they break up each section for you. They'll have a section for your title, opening, main points, and your conclusion. You can type these into your entry and adjust as needed for a completed entry.

There are also a variety of different techniques to help you with your writing. Two that I like to use often are the 10x3 matrix and WWHW technique.

The 10x3 matrix works well for blog posts where you quickly list 10 ideas or main topics and then try to think of 3 things to say about the topic (you can also use less than 10 for shorter posts).

The **WWHW** technique helps you by asking the following questions. Firstly, your introductory sentence answers the question

Why? So here you can explain why it is important or why you feel you need to address this.

The second W is the question

What? Here you will give more detail on the topic and explain the facts.

Thirdly, you will answer the

How? This might be the meat of your post and be in bullet or step form explaining how to do something in detail.

Finally, you have your closing, where you will explain the

"what if" or "what then". And this will be the result of what you have discussed.

Content Creation Tip #3: How to create content so that it can be re-used

You can create content in such a way that it can be easily reused in different formats.

The easiest way to do this is to start by creating your outline in a text editor. This can be done on any device as all devices have some sort of text editor. Text files can easily be shared and emailed around.

You can then open this txt file in a presentation program and if you have placed tabs in front of your sub-points in your text file, you will have this as bullet points in your slides. This makes slide and presentation creation quick and stress-free.

You can also open the same txt file in a word processing program and save it as a document file to create and format your posts.

From these documents you can either speak your idea with your slides and then get it transcribed or write your post out and then do audio. Either way, you will end up with both document and audio that you can turn into video to share on video sharing sites. Share your posts and articles on blogging platforms; share your slides on Slide Share.

Another good way to reuse your content is to dissect it and share parts of it on different platforms. You can share a sentence on Twitter, create a quote image for Pinterest and Instagram from a line in your article, or share a paragraph or idea on Facebook, LinkedIn or Google+.

By using this method, you will be able to reach out to more people on different platforms and sites to draw them back to your content and website.

Content Creation Tip #4: Creating content on your iPhone, iPad or other smartphone

What can't iPad and iPhones do these days? With the help of apps, you can create content, images, and information to share with the world!

The best thing you can do is to look into your phone or tablet apps as their content and abilities are always changing and adapting. It seems like they come out with a new one every year!

Be sure to check out support for information on how to transfer or upload your content to your favorite sites and information.

As technology evolves, you must learn to evolve as well and stay on top of the times. Using these ideas and latest technology, you will be able to reach out to more people and to draw them to your content.

Content Creation Tip #5: Creating Images

When it comes to social media platforms, it is important to have good visual aids to work with and to draw people in. Do you remember back in school when you had to make visual aids for each of your presentations? In a way, it's a lot like that in that having great images consistent with branding will help draw people in.

If you need help with appropriate images, stock photos, and other images can be found online for a fairly inexpensive price. You can use and reuse these images as needed.

One helpful site is called Canva, it helps you create great social media post images as well as images for your writing and other needs. If you share your final product on Pinterest and another person pins it then it helps you get attention as it leads the person right back to your page!

Pic Monkey is another great help as it allows you to edit the image at will.

Many of these images can also be edited in image hosting sites as many of them offer basic photo editing options. Manipulating the image can help you out greatly in creating unique images. Some of them will allow you to add text, quotes, and other odds and ends that you can think of to make your image unique.

If you don't have the time to edit your photo yourself, you can go to sites like Fiverr and have someone there edit your image for you or create images from scratch at an affordable price.

YOUR GUIDE TO CONTENT CREATION SUCCESS

Here is the how-to guide to create your content fast and efficiently. By following these steps, you can create in remarkably short time.

Step #1: For every theme identified in your planning session, start to investigate interesting topics

After deciding on your theme for the week or weeks, you can use the same techniques to find specific topics to write about. You can again go back to forums or podcasts in your niche or Amazon books your audience is interested in and identify more specific ideas that you wish to discuss.

Choosing a topic to write on is one of the most important things you can do. You can't begin an entry without it. Once you choose what topic you want to write on you can then begin to do your research on your topic.

If you aren't certain what topics to start on, try writing down all your ideas and what topics you might enjoy writing about.

Remember to do this in bulk and to identify topics for all of the posts that you want to create.

Step #2: Decide on the type of posts you want to write

As discussed before, there are numerous types of or ideas for posts or articles that you can write. To be honest, Digital Marketers Lab has an infographic on their website with 212 different blog post ideas. Now that can get a little overwhelming, so I mostly stick with my favorites. They include the following:

- List Posts
- FAQ or SAQ (frequently asked or should ask questions)
- Ultimate Guide Posts/How to
- Review Post
- Product Tips
- Interview
- Series

The type of post will determine the outline that you need to create. If you use a template that might already be done for you. Create the outlines or get the templates for each of the posts that you are going to create.

Step #3: Use a template or one of my techniques to start creating content fast

Alternatively, or in combination with templates, you can use the 10x3 matrix or the WWHW technique to create the meat of your content. Use the questions to expand on the topics and write 2-3 sentences on each of the topics.

Do not edit your work while you are writing. In fact, turn your spelling checker off. And get your ideas out on paper. When everything has been said, you can go back and do your editing.

Do this for all of the posts that you are writing in your blocked off time.

Step #4: Start to think how you can re-use this content

Considering the ideas discussed before on repurposing your content, decide how you are going to create content and in what different formats you would want to repurpose it.

Doing this simple step will help save you time and make the sharing of your information far easier and will help you achieve a farther reach when sharing your entries with people. Doing this will help attract people to you, your website, blog, and expertise.

Step #5: Create your branded images

The final step in content creation is the creation of images—either as stand-alone posts for Pinterest or Instagram, quotes for Facebook or complimentary to your blog posts.

As explained before, you can get good quality stock photos online or use your own photos. You can add text or quotes to them and use specific key words to help yourself get noticed. Always add your branding logo and website.

Remember Pic Monkey and Canva are helpful sites to help you create great branded images, quote posts and images for blog posts through simple editing techniques.

If you don't have the time to create your own branded image you can go to a site like Fiverr and have someone edit the image for you.

Remember that images are really important to set the mood of your content. You want to build engagement with your content, so encourage the sharing of your content by having great graphics.

PART 3: CONTENT SCHEDULING

WHY DO YOU NEED TO SCHEDULE OR AUTOMATE YOUR CONTENT?

Automating some of the more repetitive tasks related to social media can help you be more productive and efficient with the execution of your content plan.

To save you time and to improve your content marketing efforts, we can consider each of the different platforms to determine which of those tasks can be automated to create time to do the tasks that can't be automated.

Facebook

You can automate 1-2 posts per day to your Facebook page. This can include publishing your blog feed automatically or identifying trending content to add to your schedule or queue.

You can also use paid ads to promote content, increase awareness and offer discounts on an ongoing automated basis.

This will give you time to respond to fans in real time and to engage with your audience in groups. Remember to always tag people or pages when you mention them.

Twitter

You need to publish a variety of content to Twitter every day. This can all be scheduled ahead of time. You can create queues and schedule blog posts and images to Twitter more than once.

You can use a monitoring or aggregating tool to monitor keywords and mentions, to retweet influencers and to follow new people every day.

Again, this will open up your time to respond to tweets and mentions live.

LinkedIn

You can schedule posts to LinkedIn to go out a few times a week. You can also use the monitoring tools to scan industry groups a few times a week.

You can update your company profile and research prospects.

Instagram

There is no tool to automatically share to Instagram. You can use Latergramme to make it semi-automatic. You need to post to Instagram every day and also engage with your followers on a daily basis.

Pinterest

You need to share pins to your boards every day. Make sure these pins link back to your website. You can automate some parts of this and use tools to share.

Make sure to follow new boards each week and add boards that clients will be interested in.

Google+

Share your content and blog posts to Google+ a few times a week automatically. You should also promote posts from influencers in your industry. Make these posts public and circle new people regularly.

YouTube

You need to upload videos to YouTube at least weekly. This can be done manually but then you can automate tweets and Facebook posts to go out automatically sharing your videos on other platforms.

Create videos to display your expertise, to answer questions from your audience or showcase testimonials you received.

Subscribe to influencers' YouTube channels and share videos.

CONTENT AUTOMATION/SCHEDULING BASICS

Bloggers, social media marketers and online entrepreneurs all want one thing: to attract clients. An easy way to do this is to have content scheduled so that posts appear automatically.

In this section I will provide you with information regarding some of the scheduling tools. I will touch on how to get the most out of trending topics, what type of postings you should consider and how to share content from one platform to another. I will provide you with insights as to analytics and Facebook page insights and will explain why having share buttons on your site is crucial.

Throughout this section I will be providing you with valuable tips, which will not only improve your reach but will also streamline your approach, thus making the amount of time you spend online more effective as well as enjoyable. The rule of thumb here is to work smarter and not harder.

Fundamental #1: Using scheduling Tools

As mentioned earlier, the use of scheduling tools is fundamental when it comes to the streamlining of any online marketing campaign. That said, one must bear in mind that there is a huge number of scheduling tools available when it comes to automation. Some are better than others. Some offer analytics, some place limitations on length of post or how many posts one can schedule at any given time. Some tools are free while others are not.

The important thing is to find the right program that works for you. Through simple planning and the implementation of scheduling tools, you can take even the most basic marketing approach and turn it into a successful masterpiece. Scheduling content will save you both time and energy, time that can be used more efficiently to concentrate on other aspects of your marketing campaign.

Why would one make use of scheduling? The answer to that is simple. You can maximize your reach by targeting a specific audience at a precise time.

Let's assume the majority of your customer base lives in a different time zone. Rather than sit up until midnight waiting for them to come online, you can set your content to be released at a pre-determined time. We can take that one step further with the following hypothetical example.

Say you want to target a specific group. Your research tells you the target audience reflects an online presence of weekends only.

It is a given that any content posted from Monday to Friday would thus be wasted on them. However, by setting up the post to be released on weekends (and even at a specific time), you stand a much better chance of reaching your targeted audience. This will give you a definite advantage over your competitors and ultimately will lead to more customers, increased sales and additional revenue.

One of my favorite tools for this, and one which appeals to a great number of Twitter users, is the free platform TweetDeck. TweetDeck allows for several Twitter accounts and can be linked to your Facebook profile as well as any number of Facebook Pages that you admin. There is no limitation on the number of tweets or posts you can schedule. Although this is a great tool, it has its drawbacks in that it can get quite confusing when deciding which page, profile or account you wish to make use of. Another drawback is that it does not provide in depth insights that one can get when using the paid for versions of platforms such as Hootsuite or Hubspot.

My top tip for any social media posting is the use of hashtags. These tags are followed by online communities and, once you have identified those that are pertinent to your needs, can be tremendously powerful. They are used on Google +, Twitter, Instagram and Facebook. A word of caution though. Do not overdo it. Nothing is more off-putting than #reading #posts #where #every

#single #word #is #proceeded #with #a #hashtag. Don't do it. Just don't!

Fundamental #2: Leverage Trending Topics

Now that you understand the importance of hashtags and the scheduling of your posts at a specific time, we can look at how effective planning can be used to your advantage so as to get leverage out of trending topics.

Facebook, Twitter and Google + all offer information on what is trending. There are different approaches to each of these platforms according to what they offer. Let us examine each in turn.

Facebook tends to group content according to a specified topic or link. Anyone familiar with this platform will have seen posts along the lines of "Jason and five others shared the following link." By commenting on this post and providing links to our own sites, we are able to get a ton of mileage for FREE! If our posts are relevant, we are able to build trust among potential clients and to grow our own pages respectively.

Example. Jason and 5 others posted the following link (top ten Christmas carols of all time)

Our comment: "Love this post! If you are wondering what to get your loved ones for Christmas this year, why not check out what we have in our store?" (With a link to our merchandise listing).

My top tip – don't be shy to comment on other pages. Post links to your website in relevant groups. The more people who see your content, the more likely they are to visit your page. A word of caution though! Don't be spammy. Keep it relevant. Don't post adverts for funky sunglasses in a group dedicated to cancer sufferers.

Twitter gives us way more scope than Facebook in terms of targeting a specific audience. We are able to see worldwide trends, which can be broken down into regions and even cities. Once a post is trending, interest levels in the subject increase dramatically. People come online to see what it's all about. This additional interest gives marketers a chance to get extra exposure but also acts as a double edged sword. What we post could end up getting drowned out among all the "noise" of the conversation.

My favorite tip for Twitter trends is to use **Hootlet** from Hootsuite. It can be added as a free extension to your browser or be used as a stand-alone app. Hootlet basically helps us to compose a Tweet or Facebook post. It provides tips as to length of Tweet, the efficacy of your hashtag etc.

Google+ tends to be a bit trickier than either Facebook or Twitter. Trends do not show up on the main page. That does not mean they are not relevant. By making use of Google Trends, we are able to determine more specific information such as the number of posts concerning any given search criteria. Google trends also displays other relevant information such as regional interest and provides a comparison of the search criteria over a period of time.

To put the above in a nutshell, by watching for trends, we are able to determine our approach regarding content creation and according to which topics we are able to weigh in on. This helps us to plan ahead. We can schedule posts around major holidays and big events happening locally or internationally. It allows us to connect our page to the conversation with content that is relevant and to take advantage of what these trends have to offer.

Fundamental #3: Schedule a variety of post types and categories

It goes without saying that variety is key. Your posts need to be varied so as to maintain a level of interest from your audience. Here you will use the different categories of posts as discussed before and schedule about 20% of your content in each of the categories. Remember these categories include education, engagement, entertainment, inspiration and promotion.

Inside these categories you also have a variety of different type of posts e.g. List posts, how to post, FAQ posts etc.

If you keep to this, your posts will naturally only be promotional 20% of the time.

SCHEDULING/AUTOMATION TIPS YOU NEED TO KNOW

The following tips will provide you with invaluable information.

Content Automation Tip #1: Check your analytics on a continual basis

A regular check of your analytics and page insights will allow you to determine if your blog or page has gained traction over the course of a given period. It allows you to determine what is working and what is not.

By implementing the above, you can figure out what aspects of your campaign need fine tuning. Are you marketing your information to the correct gender, age group etc? Are you attracting people with valuable content or are you driving them off with boring, irrelevant information?

Once you have determined what is working, you can dedicate more time to winning posts; posts which will grow your audience through shares and which will prove to be beneficial in terms of increased readership and added sales.

eClincher is a good social media and scheduling tool that can also integrate with your analytics account and give you an all in one dashboard.

Content Automation Tip #2: Use IFTTT and Zapper to automate sharing from one platform to another

IFTTT allows you to integrate the various apps that you use. It allows for faster scheduling and the ability to keep your marketing team in sync. The beauty of IFTTT is that it integrates smoothly with cloud based storage and comes with a very nifty task manager solution.

By using IFTT and/or Zapper, you can integrate your social media so that it will automatically post from your blog to Facebook or LinkedIn. Or if you post something on YouTube it will tweet it out. You need to set this up so that it doesn't become too much, but some automation on this level is definitely an advantage.

Content Automation Tip #3: Make sure you have social sharing buttons on your website platform

You need to place sharing buttons on your blog site so that visitors can share your posts to their social media platforms. This is important because when information is shared in this manner, the third party sees the information as having come from a friend, a reliable and trusted source.

Site owners are able to determine which sites the information is being shared to, e.g. Facebook, Twitter etc. With this knowledge available, marketers can apply campaigns more effectively by focusing their attention on the site concerned.

Share buttons also contribute to the site's overall SEO rankings. Shared data provides quantifiable links, which Google relies on when rating your site.

Last, but not least, is the ease of use of share buttons. They take the hassle out of logging into your social media account, going back to the website, copying the URL, going back to the social media account, pasting the URL etc. Because these social share buttons are so simple to use, their popularity helps build brand awareness, online presence and social influence. They are a winner!

YOUR GUIDE TO CONTENT SCHEDULING SUCCESS

Finally, we are going to learn the steps needed to schedule and automate our content successfully. We have come a long way in planning and creating high quality content and the final steps will schedule these posts so that we can share it with the world and attract traffic—and, ultimately, our ideal clients—back to our website and our offerings.

Step #1: Decide which tool or tools you are going to use

There are a lot of different tools that you can use to firstly schedule your content out and secondly monitor your mentions and engagements. You need to decide what will be the best for your situation and pocket.

My favorites are CoSchedule, MeetEdgar, eClincher, Hootsuite or Buffer depending on what you need to do. Some of these tools have been discussed before and, of course, new tools come on to the market daily, so the best advice is to stay ahead of the game by keeping your ears open for the latest tools.

A tool like eClincher is an all in one tool with which you can engage with all of your platforms from one central dashboard. You can monitor your mentions, your competition or any other keywords that you might be interested in and also create questions for content in different categories to automatically go out at pre-selected times.

Step #2: Setup automated scheduling in IFTTT and other tools

Besides having one tool to schedule your posts to different media platforms, you can also link your Rss feed and different platforms with the help of IFTTT. Just keep in mind where you've already scheduled your content so that you don't overdo it.

Step #3: With your planner in hand, start to schedule your blog posts first

Once you have all your tools set up and linked, you can start scheduling your blog posts for the allocated time. You can use CoSchedule or the WordPress native scheduler to do this. eClincher will also have the ability to schedule to WordPress and Tumblr in the next release.

Step #4: Share your blog posts to other platforms if not automatically done

Your blog post should automatically go out to Facebook, Twitter, Google+ and LinkedIn. Depending on the software you use, you might have to manually share your posts to Pinterest, YouTube or Instagram. Also post your newly created post in other Facebook groups or forums.

You can either have your RSS feed setup to send out an email automatically or you need to send out a newsletter informing your audience of your new post.

Step #5: Schedule more content to different platforms

Now that your blog posts are scheduled, and you have set up automatic sharing of your posts, you can add more posts and content to your schedule and queues.

As said before, try to add a variety of different types of posts in the 5 different categories. You can use a tool like MeetEdgar or eClincher to have a bucket or category and then, randomly or in order, publish content from these buckets.

Step #6: With everything else automated, you can now monitor and engage at scheduled times each day

You now have everything ready to go out. The only thing left to do is to schedule some time each day for live engagements and monitoring of mentions and keywords or hashtags if you want to. Using tools to help you have everything in one place can reduce time spent on this even more.

WHY IS CREATING CONTENT IMPORTANT?

In the Digital Information Age, content is not only 'king,' it's the global currency we use to communicate and transact online with each other.

Your business needs content for website pages, blog, newsletters, product descriptions, post headlines, sales copy, social media, ads, articles, promotional pieces, news releases, customer training, FAQs, forum signatures, SEO (e.g. meta descriptions), etc.

Publishing content online helps your business:

- Drive traffic to your website and social media pages

- Keep your website relevant in the search engines

- Educate prospects about your products and services

- Turn visitors into customers and subscribers

- Keep visitors, subscribers, clients, and online users engaged

- Train new clients/customers, staff members, subscribers, resellers, affiliates, etc.

- Build trust, authority, and credibility

- Stay ahead of the competition

- And much more.

Knowing how to create good content, then, is one of the most valuable skills you can have for growing a business online.

Creating quality content regularly, however, is challenging. You need a content marketing strategy, a plan, and a system for coming up with new ideas and turning these into published content.

Content Ideas Are Infinite

In reality, there's no shortage of content ideas. In fact, there is an **infinite** supply of ideas. If content ideas were finite, the arts, news, and entertainment industry would already have ceased to exist. There would be no more songs to compose, books or plays to write, dances to be choreographed, movies to be made, news to report, or courses to teach because all of these require content.

Most people, however, get stuck when it comes to coming up with new ideas and don't publish content often enough.

Not being able to come up with new ideas and not publishing content regularly are two different issues and we'll address these separately later.

If you're not publishing content regularly, your business is missing out on many opportunities like:

- Gaining more online business exposure/mindshare.

- Attracting more visitors and generating more leads and potential customers.

- Winning more business and making more sales.

- Generating more subscribers, members, etc.

- Saving time answering commonly asked questions.

- Saving time on customer support and training.

- Establishing your expertise and authority in your industry or niche.

- Building credibility and trust with people who may be interested in your products or services.

- Being seen or perceived as a business that keeps up-to-date with the latest developments.

- Staying relevant in your industry or niche.

- Getting ahead of your competition.

- And more!

The good news is that you can easily overcome these challenges and take advantage of these opportunities.

Content Is An Asset

If you don't think publishing content on your website is an asset, take a look at the share prices of companies that depend entirely on content like Google and Facebook.

If sites did not publish content that online users are searching for, Google would not have a search engine and miss out on billions of dollars in advertising.

Facebook is built entirely out of user-generated content. No content, no Facebook.

Content, then, is a valuable asset that can:

- Build up the value of your website/online business and increase its resale value.

- Be re-purposed to create new assets (i.e. new digital products).

- Help you generate additional revenue.

- Improve the effectiveness of your sales process.

- And more.

If you're trying to grow a business online, every new article you publish can act like a salesperson that never goes to sleep, never gets sick or takes days off, and is continually working 24/7 to promote your business, products, or services.

It's important, then, to treat content as an asset and to understand that the content creation process allows you to keep producing more valuable assets.

Content Gives You A Competitive Advantage

The same challenges that stop you from creating and publishing content regularly are also stopping your competitors from growing **their** business online.

Most businesses – especially small businesses – don't create or publish content regularly. They have no content strategy or processes for coming up with new ideas and turning these into published content.

Many businesses, in fact, have bought into the idea that their website is just an 'online brochure' to make them appear more credible to prospects, so they go no further than adding a few basic web pages about who they are and what they do and maybe occasionally publishing an article or blog post. These websites get no benefit or leverage from content marketing.

In today's global digital economy, if you don't understand the power of content marketing, you run the risk of being left behind by competitors who do.

Creating and publishing content regularly, then, helps you build an asset and gain a competitive advantage.

CONTENT WRITING TIPS

Now that we've looked at why creating content is important, let's start with some basic writing tips.

There are only two hurdles when it comes to creating content for your website or blog:

1) Overcoming the idea that you are "too busy" to create and publish content regularly.

2) Knowing what to write about.

We need three things to overcome these hurdles:

1) Change our mindset from "I can't think of anything to write about" to "there's just so much to write about,"

2) Develop a content strategy to answer the **whats**, **whys**, and **hows** of our content creation efforts,

3) Implement an effective system for the production of regular content.

In other words, what we need is a **system** that will help us automate the process of coming up with new ideas, making sure that these ideas fit our strategy, and getting these into production.

Before we look at some tips to help us do this, let's start with some facts:

1) There is an infinite supply of ideas. If you learn where to look and are open to receiving these, you will never run out of new content ideas.

2) Ideas are just thoughts until they materialize into form. Coming up with lots of ideas is a great start but in order to create results, you'll need to take action to turn thoughts and ideas into something concrete.

Just as we can't start furnishing a room until we have a house with rooms, the first thing we need to do is build a house. This will be the foundation that will help us materialize our ideas into form. Once this foundation is laid, we can then begin to unlock the "infinite content generator" in our brain, so that as new ideas start flowing, we will be able to harness, channel, process, and turn these into published content.

Tip #1: Everyone Is Also *"Too Busy" … Just Get Started!*

We only have 24 hours a day. And we're all using every one of these 24 hours every single day.

The only way we can get more done in the time we have, then, is to work **smarter**.

Systems help you work smarter. Good systems let you leverage your time and your efforts, so you get more done with less time and less effort.

If you start thinking about **everything** in terms of systems, you will be able to get more done and achieve more using the same amount of time everyone else gets.

Let's start thinking about **content creation**, then, as a system!

Let's start with your business. Do you find that different prospects often ask you the same questions over and over again, or that customers contact you about the same issues, challenges, or problems?

Many of these questions take prospects only seconds to ask but they take us minutes or even hours to explain. How much time and productivity are we wasting answering the same questions and explaining the same things over and over again?

Have you heard the saying that everyone who approaches your business is a **suspect** until they qualify as a **prospect**? Many of the questions we find ourselves answering over and over again aren't coming from prospects but **suspects**.

Think of all the extra time and productivity your business would gain if it had:

1) A system for separating suspects and 'tire kickers' who are merely curious about your business from genuine prospects and customers, and

2) A system for dealing respectfully with all three types of people (suspects, prospects, and customers or clients) so that everyone gets the information and the answers they are looking for.

We can easily use content to create this system.

First, you would set up a **planning process** to create different sections in your website where new pages can be added with information specifically targeting each group your business deals with on a regular basis. This includes suspects, prospects, customers or clients, staff, subscribers, members, suppliers, resellers, etc.

Next, you would set up an **information gathering process** to record, store, organize, and retrieve all the questions, objections, complaints, etc. that your business receives on a regular basis.

Finally, you would set up a **content production process** for turning this information into new articles, tutorials, blog posts, videos, etc. that will then get published on your site, social media pages, etc.

Now you have a system that you and everyone in your business can use to direct suspects, prospects, customers or clients, staff, subscribers, members, suppliers, resellers, and everyone else you deal with. Each of these groups can find the answers they are looking for, do research, or learn more about your business and your products or services in **their** own time, not yours!

If you were to commit just a few hours each week to build a system that can save your business hundreds of hours each week or thousands of hours every month or every year, wouldn't this be working smarter? Wouldn't this give you more leverage, improve your productivity, streamline your efficiency, and help you get better results?

All of this can be done using inexpensive tools and processes and it won't take you long to do it. If you spend 4 hours each week putting a system like this in place, once the system is built, you then have 4 hours a week to spend on creating content for your website or blog, plus the leverage of your system and all of the content being added to it.

But ... What If I Really Don't Have Time To Write Content?

Most people are busy and want things done for them. I don't blame you for wanting to skip ahead to the part where we talk about outsourcing your content creation.

The problem is that if you skip the lessons on how to put processes in place to outsource effectively, you will not save time or money. In fact, it will probably cost you more time and more money and you will end up disappointed with the results.

Regardless of whether you plan to write your own content or have it outsourced, you will still need to invest time into planning, systems, and processes to control not just the quality of the work but how the content is produced, created, and delivered to your expectations and specifications, especially if you want to publish quality information online.

Creating content is challenging and time-consuming and so is managing the content creation process. The only way to overcome these challenges and save time is to invest some time upfront into putting effective systems and processes in place.

SUMMARY

Avoid making the common mistake of thinking that you will start publishing content on your website when you have spare time. Who has time to spare? No one. Every business owner you'll ever meet is already using all 24 hours of their day.

You will save time if you begin to think of content creation as a system and have systems in place to create content. You will then be able to work smarter by directing visitors, prospects, customers, staff, suppliers, subscribers, etc. to the content on your website instead of spending time unnecessarily answering the same questions or explaining the same things to different people.

ACTION STEP

Don't let the excuse of being "too busy" prevent you from creating and implementing an effective content creation system that will help to free up your time, boost your productivity, improve efficiency, and help you get better results.

Schedule 2-4 hours every week to focus on your content creation processes. Begin by using this scheduled time to go through the lessons in this course and develop your content strategy and content plan. Once this is done, use the same time slot to begin implementing your strategy and putting systems in place. After this, use the same time slot to create content – either by doing it yourself or managing the process of getting it done.

Tip #2: You Don't Need To Be A Writer

An excuse that prevents many website owners from regularly creating and publishing content is "I'm not a writer."

You don't need to be a writer to publish content online about your business or about something you have a passion or interest in.

I have no formal training as a writer. In fact, English isn't even my native language. Yet, I have been creating and publishing content online almost every day for over a decade now. I have published many articles and blog posts, written hundreds of tutorials, dozens of online guides and e-books, created online courses, videos, slide presentations, etc. and I still can't stop coming up with new content ideas.

You don't need to be a writer. As far as this course is concerned, your audience is not looking for literary masterpieces with flawless grammar and punctuation. That's not who you're writing content for. You're writing content to attract and engage audiences that are searching for your products and services and publishing content that will help your business grow online and stay one step ahead of your competitors.

Once you understand what kind of information your audience is searching for, have systems in place to create and deliver it, and unlock the "Infinite Content Creation" generator in your brain to keep coming up with more ideas for web content, you won't even think of this as 'writing' anymore. It will just become a part of what you need to do to help your audience and grow your business.

Here's what I suggest you think about when you think about 'writing' content …

Think about whatever it is that you do in your business or line of work or whatever it is that you have an interest or passion for.

Most people have no difficulty talking about what they do or what they are interested in or passionate about. In fact, some people can easily talk for hours on end about the things they know about to anyone willing to listen.

In essence, all you are really doing when blogging or creating content for your website is "talking about your business" in writing.

Just write the way you would normally talk to a prospect or someone who's really interested in what you do if you were having a one-on-one conversation with them at a business event or at a social function.

Think about how you would educate them about the unique aspects or qualities of your business; the unique benefits and advantages of your products or services; what problems you help people solve; how you help improve or add value to other people's lives, why people need your products or services, etc.

By focusing on how you would talk to people about your business, passion, or interest if you were helping them instead of worrying about "how to write," you will be educating more prospects to do business with you and training more customers or clients to become better users of your products or services. You will also build more credibility, authority, and trust with visitors and improve your chances of becoming the "go-to" expert in your field or the leading solution provider in your industry or niche.

SUMMARY

You don't need to be a writer to create and publish great web content. Just focus on educating and helping people and "talk about your business" in writing.

ACTION STEP

Recall a recent conversation you've had with someone (i.e. a prospect, customer, or client) about your business, products, or services, where you were asked a question or were met with an objection.

Write this question or objection down.

Now, imagine that you have just met your ideal prospect or client and they have just asked you the same question or stated the same objection. How would you reply? What would you say to leave them feeling 100% satisfied with your answer?

If you want to, you can also play "devil's advocate" for this exercise and imagine coming across the 'worst' ideal prospect you'll ever meet. Imagine all the hard and difficult questions they would ask and all the issues or objections they would raise, and how you would answer their questions and address their objections and concerns to win them over.

Now, here is the important part ...

Write down exactly what you would say in the exact way you would say it. Don't edit or polish anything in your answer just yet. Just write everything down. Once you're done, go over what you have just written and note how long it's taken you to write it all down.

Congratulations ... you have just **talked about your business in writing!** All you need to do now to turn this into great web content is tidy things up a little bit, then put yourself in your ideal prospect's shoes and see how it all reads back to you.

When you're happy with the results, publish it as an article on your website or blog.

Develop a habit of practicing having imaginary conversations, presentations, or Q&A sessions with your ideal prospects, customers, or clients, and you will soon find yourself writing and blogging about your business (or passion or interest) on a regular basis.

Tip #3: Write As You Would Normally Speak

You don't need to try to be clever, witty, or entertaining when you write or blog about your business.

Just write as you would normally speak.

For example, pick a typical problem or challenge that your customers often experience and address this in your article or blog post using your normal voice and manner of speaking. Write down the exact words you would use.

Read some of what you've written aloud. Does it sound like you? If so, great! If not, make it sound like you! Continue doing this as you talk about the benefits and advantages of your products or services and how these specifically address the problem or challenge. Provide tips that will help make their buying decision easier and explain what kind of results new customers can expect to get or what kind of after sales service, support, or training they can expect to receive.

Just be yourself as you write the above. Imagine how you would speak if you were engaging one-on-one with a very happy (or even an irate) prospect, customer, or client, and write everything down in your normal style of conversation using your own words.

As you write things down, also think about the order you would say things to your prospects or clients. For example, if you normally start off by describing the problem first, what causes the problem, and how your solutions help to address the problem, then arrange your answer to match this structure. This will not only help you write better content, it will also help to improve your sales process.

SUMMARY

Just as you were asked to talk about your business in writing, just write things down the way you would normally speak.

ACTION STEP

Write down a typical response to a frequently asked question exactly as you would normally speak. Save your answer somewhere where you can easily find it and don't do anything else for now.

*** Do it now ***

Have you done this? If you haven't, please stop reading and do it right now ... it should only take you a few minutes.

If you have done this, great! We'll come back to it after the next tip.

Now that we know why content creation is so integral to the process of creating profitable blogs and how to create stellar content, let's look at how you can widen your reach and draw an even bigger audience to your blog by using these highly actionable content marketing strategies.

1. Guest Blogging

One of the easiest and most effective ways to spread the word about your blog and come off as more authoritative at the same time is to write guest blog posts. You find similar blogs in your niche or popular industry websites and create insightful posts for them.

Make it well-researched, detailed and analytical to position yourself as an expert on the subject. You will not just end up building brand authority but also draw a swarm of traffic to your blog. Include a link to your blog in the author bio along with a power-packed description.

2. Social Media Ads

Social ads are a good way to gain some traction for your posts. You do not need to throw away hundreds of dollars on promoting your blog. Even a post boost of $15-20 can help you gain decent exposure if you have put out amazingly share-worthy content. Ads (especially Facebook ads) give you a very large yet focused audience.

3. Do not Be Overtly Promotional

Do not be overtly promotional when it comes to content marketing. Remember the purpose is to take your reader/potential buyer through a buying cycle. Do not go full throttle, jet boating on your customers immediately. Let them gain some value before you start seeking conversions.

4. Start with a Framework

You may not always have products or services to talk about, especially in the earlier stages of the blog. Skip the product/service talk and focus on a larger framework (that impacts readers) that deals with themes, ideas and issues. Keep the topics closely connected and relevant to your target audience.

5. Do not Monetize Until You Rank

Garnering links to your posts can be really tough. Make it simpler by not combining your content marketing (drawing an audience to your blog) with monetizing efforts. Do not undertake any money-making activity until you rank well. Once you have undertaken sufficient outreach activities, rank well, and draw a decent audience of regular readers, only then start your monetization methods. Do not ruin your blog's long-term chances by trying to make a few quick bucks from your blog early on.

Of course, you may not have the luxury to wait until you make money. People need quick returns to meet their expenses. If you can afford to hold off earning from your blog (until you rank well for competitive keywords and draw a decent traffic), you can gain a lot more in the long run.

6. Leverage Email Campaigns

Much as new-age internet marketers would have you believe otherwise, email campaigns are far from dead. Emails continue to play a vital role in the process of generating traffic for your blog.

Send interesting, informative and content rich newsletters to your email subscribers. Integrate content into a logical sales funnel that compels your target audience to buy. For instance, if you are selling some products related to baby nutrition, try to offer some tips or recipes related to nutrition.

Establish your expertise in the field of child nutrition and get readers to trust you by populating their email feed with valuable and useful content.

7. Connect with Influencers

Create a list of influencers within your industry using a tool like Little Bird. Use social media to connect with them. Cross promote each other's blogs. Retweet the content of popular influencers for them to notice you and follow your blog, and eventually share your content among their followers.

Get them to write guest posts for you and share links to the post on their social media pages. This way their hundreds of followers will find you and start following you too.

8. Create Evergreen Content

Evergreen content are pieces that stay relevant irrespective of its time of publication. You can create tons of free how-to guides and small reports that remain relevant to your audience, which saves you the hassle of updating the content periodically.

9. Use Your Best Headlines for Pay Per Click Ads

If you are using PPC campaigns to promote your blog, repurpose your best-performing headlines into an attention-grabbing ad copy. If you realized that a headline worked particularly well with your target audience, repurpose into your ad copy. There really isn't much difference between blog post content and PPC ads regarding the angles that are used to hook readers/customers (such as emotionally tugging angles, strong action verbs, and clear benefits). If you are not sure between different set of headlines, run A/B test to gauge how each headline is performing individually. You will know what types of headlines or content ad copy resonates best with your audience.

10. Keep it Consistent with Your Brand Voice

Content marketing is the best way to develop, refine and reinforce your brand/blog's voice. However, even the biggest brands fail to identify their voice or clearly define it.

Ensure that your content reflects the consistency and continuity of your brand. Review your editorial stands periodically to ascertain that the tone and voice of your brand are consistent with the blog persona in general. Are you positioning yourself as a fun, youthful, fresh blog for a younger audience? Are you positioning yourself as an authoritative and serious source of information in your industry?

While drafting or marketing each post, ask how the content can advance you blog's persona, goals or value? What does the tone of your blog reflect? Does it reinforce your company's values?

11. Answer Complex Questions Using Long Tail Keywords

Attempt to answer complicated questions related to your niche with more targeted and specific, long-tail keywords. You will increase your chances of ranking for a larger number of more focused keywords, where customers are actively seeking information.

While some content creators and marketers believe in writing naturally without adopting a keyword-based approach, others strongly advocate targeting your audience with long tail or more focused keywords. Before creating content that you are using for boosting your content marketing efforts, make a comprehensive list of the keywords you are looking to rank for.

By doing a quick scan or survey of some popular forums within your industry, you will know exactly what your readers are looking for. Make dedicated and detailed posts for addressing these queries and post them of these forums (if permitted). You can also leave lots of smart tips or ideas or little-known information on these forum threads and include a link to your blog in the author bio.

CONCLUSION

I sincerely hope the book was able to help you gain insights into the process of content creation for running a highly profitable blog.

The next step is to stop planning and start taking action. There are tons of little-known tips, tried and tested strategies and actionable wisdom nuggets for helping blog publishers build their blog content, increase their authority and establish an equation of trust with potential buyers. From beginners to seasoned blog publishers and marketers, everyone can benefit from the easy-to-follow yet insanely effective strategies discussed in this book.

Finally, if you enjoyed reading the book, please take some time out to share your thoughts by posting a review on Amazon. It would be highly appreciated.

Here's to being a highly successful blog publisher!

www.ingramcontent.com/pod-product-compliance
Ingram Content Group UK Ltd.
Pitfield, Milton Keynes, MK11 3LW, UK
UKHW021259180426
11947UKWH00015B/928